Glimmer of Hope

KJ GoForth

Gotham Books

30 N Gould St.
Ste. 20820, Sheridan, WY 82801
https://gothambooksinc.com/

Phone: 1 (307) 464-7800

© 2023 KJ GoForth. All rights reserved.

No part of this book may be reproduced, stored in a retrieval system, or transmitted by any means without the written permission of the author.

Published by Gotham Books (March 23, 2023)

ISBN: 979-8-88775-219-8 H
ISBN: 979-8-88775-108-5 P
ISBN: 979-8-88775-109-2 E

Because of the dynamic nature of the Internet, any web addresses or links contained in this book may have changed since publication and may no longer be valid.

The views expressed in this work are solely those of the author and do not necessarily reflect the views of the publisher, and the publisher hereby disclaims any responsibility for them.

Table of Contents

Content was provided by a few dear friends. A possible love interest. Several monopolized corporations. Some diabolical fear spreading organizations oh and more confusion than there are words on the planet.

Reference Page

An unabated conscience.

Touch me Angel and explore
The female nature that you've bore

Genuine and pure like snow
A perfect beauty with all the flow

Unique authentic rising star
Ever knowing never far

Illumination from within
Other worldly soul of kin

Hear this message stand above
Any other thing but love

Be your best self let it define
Courage craving as your shine

Inoculation presently
Feel my heart feel the need

Selfless serving greater good
Golden statue not of wood

Grace and glory to your soul
Be the one be the glow

Morning beautiful it's been so long
I've been writing a brand new song

Harps and flutes serenade
This lovely sound that's been made

Bellows fill with the air
Timeless teachings do declare

Outward sounding resonate
Years of practice worth the wait

Focused fearless out on stage
The time is now all the rage

Copycatting not my style
Living breathing with a smile

Guided ushered bring it bold
Break the curse don't let it hold

Ease the throttle not the break
Hold your head up stay awake

Bent over crying hands to the head
Feeling alone like I am dead

Time spent confused darkness surrounds
Where is my family and their beautiful sounds

Isolated and trapped out on a limb
Walking the plank sink or swim

Crashing of waves turbulent seas
Lost on an ocean violent the breeze

Chaos ensues how can it be
This should be easy I should be free

All is not just All is not fair
All is the witness All is the dare

Laughing at liars punking the punks
Greeting the grateful discernment for drunks

Bitter bastards pack your bags
Ring out your bloody negative nags

On the sunset of this day
I release my love for you so play

Our entangled souls will never die
My thoughts of you I proudly cry

Conviction thought your inner strength
Has brought me closer to the brink

Disclosure near exuberant
Here to catch your discontent

Fill your cup let it spill
Be yourself feel the thrill

Isolation has made you strong
Millions cry as you sing your song

Brilliant beauty shining through
Angelic wisdom made for two

Hidden away surface rise
To blind the people glowing eyes

Keep the glow feel the flow
Live the life only we know

Memory of her heart tearing me apart

Hostage of her love an angel from above

Legend from a myth who's lips I'll never kiss

Teardrops from the Gods universe's laws

Hypnotized by grace haven't seen her face

Tantalizing dish but I have no wish

Love already taken why my heart is breaking

Time to back it down as to not become a clown

Not this one for me still happy always free

Candy on the table only when I'm able

Open to the tease always here to please

Tossed about without doubt

Found a way start today

Sights set high wings to fly

Survey surroundings after the groundings

Was down for the count but don't count me out

Becoming a man only one fan

Crowd sits in awe from what they have saw

Brittle indeed all have the need

Costing no dough time to let go

Seek inner self improve one's health

Testimony clear don't live in fear

Guilt by accusation laying blame
Fear full of anything that's not the same

Poised to inflict tearing apart
Doing its damage no secular start

Township unholy altered by men
Focused on power where to begin

Bread to conform altered by lies
Destined to fail not a surprise

Testimony tells of heaven on earth
Come get the righteous give us new birth

Hold up your light see through the dark
Give me your hand walk in the park

Question intentions set forth in me
Make me the man I was intended to be

Tear up any contract that causes us fear
Lift up the willing who want to stay her

Empire building maintaining power
Whipping its slaves every hour

Keep warship tested generate
War Lords of kingdom perpetrate

Battle driven conquered land
Drunk with power band aid brand

Controlled illusion waves it's flag
Taking lives body bag

Sought with anger growing greed
Peasants dying no food to feed

Balloted sickness nothing else
Waves of terror not knowing self

Remove your face remove your heart
And watch all kingdoms fall apart

Beckoning call reach the top
We can do it never stop

Change is healthy but not easy
It might even leave you dizzy

What excuse will come next
Bitchy victims without sex

Narrative nothing new
Pain and suffering we should sue

Arrogant idol above the bed
Thoughts of bleeding covered red

Sole provider hasn't changed
Take a gun blow out your brain

Take the righteous leave the meek
Are the words that I speak

Right the wrongs hear my words
Come and take all these turds

Codependency growing costing freedom
Who is responsible who has been leadin'

United a joke divided its truth
Hangs on a thread tied to one tooth

Sick and dying like the church
Leave it to men to scorch the earth

Separation of church and state
Our for fathers saw our fate

Power hungry frivolous
I'll bend over you can kiss

Eat my shorts realize
I can see through all the lies

Slave no more I can see
Righteous dipshits never free

Path disturbed from its birth
Love myself and mother earth

What about druthers which way have you gone
Are you a chicken or a beautiful swan

How 'bout a goat or sheep in the herd
How 'bout a dark wolf reading the word

Intention salvation righteous its drug
Preference disgusting how 'bout a hug

Weak of the will same senseless trap
Think for yourself forget all that crap

What's wrong with love believing alone
Feel it inside you in every bone

Wash yourself pure empty your mind
Take out the trash so you're not blind

Why follow non sense fear ridden fools
Dull in the dark without sharp tools

Graceful gliding through this space
Wings spread wide fo win the race

Immense freedom from within
Strength and growth not imagine

No more egg shells confident
Big results evident

Showing passion all and is
Intuition like a wiz

Tell me why you've become so dull
Time to lighten up your hull

Confined no more time to lead
Stop the bleeding from all who bleed

Stiches and band aids won't do this time
Gash to big pours out wine

Killing free thought crooks of men
Authority on noting the true sin

Tell me tell me sing to me
Hold my heart set me free

Cast out shadows leave no doubt
Plan of plans shift and shout

Puzzle building which one next
Outstretched arms awaiting text

Who's the son what's his name
Righteous fools are insane

Free to give shining bright
With clear conscience I sleep tonight

Control creeping ever near
Maybe now it's last year

Breathe your breath infuse the soul
Revive the sleeping so we can grow

Ship of fools I'm leaving you
Emotional sections no more rules

Anchor lifted critters gone
Paradise bound holding on

No more reigns vail clear
At the helm my ship to steer

Poisoned waters left behind
Dulling image tarnished shine

No more row boat leaking hull
No fear casting battered soul

Scooba gear off found my pearl
Now it's time to shock the world

No triangle smashed the box
Circular motion freakin' rocks

Be the next find your way
Keep on trying everyday

Where's your gift horse who the boss
Don't even know what the loss

Contrived dilution shady base
Same old shit nasty face

Crucifixion martyr man
Go away not a fan

Find a cliff and hold hands
You're not welcome on these lands

Bottle in one hand book in other
Killing children and their mother

You're the poison of the land
You're the virus here I stand

Fleece the flock guide your herd
To the toilet for a turd

A light so bright must be shown
Like ET phoning home

Luke Skywalker princess lay
Use the force everyday

Superman and kryptonite
Superheroes are alright

But we're the hero of our own fate
Feeling good levitate

Dance with freedom forget the pain
Don't let chaos make its stain

It's our time to rise above
No room for fear in this glove

Earth love model kindred souls
We the boss let's let ums know

Flip the switch generate
Live in love not in hate

Turn your key find that door
Open quickly don't ignore

Walk with pride F the fear
Be your own boss not a queer

Calla coward what it is
No more shadows born to live

Grace and dignity shine within
Don't give up we have to win

Transform your dark into light
Head held high time to fight

Martyr models going down
Admit defeat or become a clown

One more scripture punching bag
What a downer what a drag

Hold out your hand she said to me
I am the magic you are the key

My kingdom is yours you are my king
I give you my honor you give me your ring

Our fate to meet right here and now
Make me your queen let's take a vow

Be the true man I've seen in my dreams
Lift me hold me carry me cross streams

My hero my lover my knight shining through
Togethers again I know it is true

A union in heaven here on this earth
I want your children I want to give birth

Pinch me hurry make sure this is real
Together forever all things can heal

Breathe into life a breath new and fresh
Send me the symbol send me the crest

Our old one is broken model worn out
Corrupted by men I have no doubt

Give me the wisdom give me strength
Fight all my battles lift me in rank

Be the provider lighten my load
Smooth out my path widen this road

My heart is yours brighten my way
Sing me your song made new everyday

Tear down the walls implode false thrones
Let the vultures peck at the bones

Omnipresent I feel you see it too
Poison the serpent who imitates you

Still in the silence show me how
Your love is eternal I trust in this vow

Motzart Bethoven Bach
Meloy stirs me like some watch the clock

Accomplished and tuned true works of art
Romantically inspired it speaks to the heart

Rooted in sound carried away
Start of each day grand stage like a play

Were these all past lives I'll never know
The melody and rhythm speak to my soul

Akoshic in nature tuned for my vibe
Glad it's still with us glad it survived

A portrait of nature stellar indeed
All has been given all that we need

This is our home we are the ones
We are responsible for our own going ons

Soulless sick and sad
Conform because your bad

Foster foreign, fires
Military buyers

Guilty gushing goo
Fearing war dejavu

Same result same foundation
Beggars cry out for redemption

Prayers unheard by the light
In the darkened halls of fright

Pushed aside buried deep
Truth residing under the heap

Burden yours not the church
Free your mind begin your search

Sun goes down one more day
So much to learn no time to play

The seriousness of where we are heading
Leaves me hopeless leave me dreading

I'll need to center balance things out
Let out frustration let out the doubt

One more test another trial
I can feel it one more mile

I can do this it's why I'm here
Don't loose sight don't have fear

Freedom and love are worth the fight
Sore above disfunction live in the light

Get some sleep tomorrow will come
A new beginning for all not some

Internal external fairytale
Moby Dick is the whale

Cinderella and snow white
One glass slipper apple fright

Japetto and Pinocchio
Master craftsman don't 'cha know

Alice and her wonderland
LSD trip out of hand

Unicorns and dragon's lair
Imagination don't you dare

Mermaids and Atlantis
Evolution and semantics

Evolved creation earth's own past
Untrapped minds free to cast

Fairytale or our truth
Imagination is your proof

When confusion gets too much
When you feel you're out of touch
When you're feeling real burnt out
When you want to scream and shout
When your sad and wanna cry
When this dream has passed on by
When you need someone to hear
When the laughter turns to tear
When all true things become a lie
When honesty set flight to fly

When truth becomes the only reason
When acts are like the changing seasons
When piece prevails through our love
When a golden heart fits like a glove
When every moment with ever thought
When wisdom fills us every spot
When creation fixes all that pain
When knowing that it's not in vain
When holding on is worth the fight
When loving bonds make us light
It's been your plan I know it's you
My heart is yours this is true

Toxic bodies toxic hearts
Toxic minds toxic farts

Incompetence ruling every phase
Hopeless homeless never praise

Energy uselessly given away
On your knees you are the prey

Empires ruling all we know
Controlling thoughts conforming soul

Tested wicked evil ways
Shameful fearful pissed off days

Butchered beliefs spreading fear
Giving pain to my rear

Sing me one sweet lullaby
Tears of joy pass on by

Time to go it's been nice
I am here to break the ice

Majestically standing courageous and tall
Cinderella at the ball

Bravery beyond any before
Showering goodness opinions ignored

Knowing a purpose buried so deep
Not tricked in believing there will be no defeat

Long felt desire no need to fit in
Awareness still growing always within

Guarded and guided treachery sustains
Intelligence compounded flows through the veins

Make no mistake no martyr this time
Witness humanity transcend to its prime

Gratitude and respect to be shown my own truth
United to greatness a wonderous a luth

Three headed dog blood of a hog

Intense in its force righteous of course

Destined to fail sward to empale

Gallop away no room to stay

Control for too long same old sad song

Blistering spine drunk on its wine

Shocking with love brought from above

Not going away we've come to stay

Beckoning brought costing a lot

Sickening sad not me I'm rad

Delirious dream writing each scene

Compromised free will justified blood spill

Beholden to a book narrated by a crook

Half and partial lies conformity denies

Manipulate the mass' burnt covered in ashes

Dead end conversation mental masturbation

Disturbing acts of terror history its bearer

Poisonous thorny spikes visionary kikes

Pedestal built on ground that isn't very sound

Talking points so weak besides what feeds the weak

Squawking to the end not time to pretend

As above so below pay your bills it's time to go

Grateful for this time
Grateful for this chance
Grateful for what needs be done
Grateful for this dance
Thankful for creation
Thankful for this life

Thankful for the lessons learnt
Thankful all despite
Gracious in the now
Optimistic in the future
Patiently waiting quietly
Resilient strength to feature
Courage to keep moving
Proud of where I've been
Recognizing unknow
Looking for my kin

Close your eyes and walk with me
Clear your mind and be free

Sleeping deep within each core
A restless giant poised to roar

Instruction written on each heart
Secret books can never start

A part of inner wisdom shines
No constraints no confines

This hostage living in the pain
Robbing us with disdain

It's your time the time is now
This inner wisdom awaits your vow

A warriors death set me free
Now nature's beauty all I see

Brought alive by this death
Sharing secrets breath by breath

This connection to a wonderous place
Her restless changing beauty grace

Creation conscious ever wise
Untold stories brutal lives

She's my leader she's our truth
Aging slowly in her youth

Pulse undying rebirth rebuild
New beginnings death concealed

Her children marvel as they play
Connection growing everyday

Respect the ground you walk upon
Cuz someday soon you will be gone

Botched beginning cruel fate
Men and lies denigrate

Soul revival wait and see
Worth the pain and misery

True in nature souring high
Bread for strength wings to fly

Wipe the tears concentrate
Free your soul liberate

Who we are where were from
Open your heart and become

Deconstruct distractions held in vain
Surrender ego release the pain

Trust the cosmos and its creed
Leave behind all that greed

Harness all of what we are
Be the evening bright ass star

No longer a victim learning to live
Taught about love willing to give

A system that's broken by polar disease
Take all these drugs and get on your knees

Quiet the voices get in line
You're not going crazy your trying to shine

Unlock your power let your love glow
Walk through the shadows into the chateau

Harness the energy seek your own truth
Let by gones be by gones trust there's real proof

Commit to a purpose and see it through
You'll be rewarded God willing love you

A crack in the cast a mold all my own
Generations of suffering time to come home
Riding the clouds free to sore
Breaking down barriers knocking in doors
Present and seeking only our truth
Content for the moment oneness aloof
Wake up in its presence lie down in its grace
Never alone smile on my face
Toil no more an iceberg at sea
Floating with freedom, freedom is me
Sovern in spirit discernment on wise
Glimpse through the vail starting to rise
Uplifting and shocking all in same breath
Deep scars healed up causing a death

Like a wolf that stocks it's prey
The weak won't get away

A dance that can't tell time
New beginning meant to shine

The breath of twisted fate
Hold steady don't be late

Darkness all around
Silent memories do astound

Carved from solid gold
Free to be so bold

Become the light and see
What we were meant to be

When the darkness clears into the light
It warms the soul my friend tonight

The calming piece that comes within
Knowing love let life begin

Washed and pure lessons learned
Closet empty cobwebs burned

Become the light and find the self
Inspire the masses free of doubt

A happy heart shines so bright
Like a light house in the night

Ward off danger with pure love
Kill with kindness no need to shove

Back to basics distracted no more
Watch me open another door

Break the cycle heal your past
Walk in rhythm shed the cast

Burn the box conform no more
Peal the layers step through the door

Bow to greatness flow within
Heart that shimmer once
again

Block the lies embrace your truth
Enter mystery child like youth

Become yourself and you will find
Life is precious so divine

No beast or burden no cross to bare
Only truth if you dare

Ride your truth fill your cup
Wash your conscience hurry up

Its truest form Awe is real
Explore the self begin to heal

A vision of life to blow the mind
Free the soul cuz now it's blind

A heart so pure revitalized
Conscience stirs conceptualize

As one life begins to bloom
Glowing bright the fullest moon

Untangled web free from the snare
Energy flowing everywhere

Bestowed each gift every life
Destined now to reach the light

Hold back nothing implode each dam
Each and ever one a lamb

A lamb that's turned into a bird
Hold fast steady every word

Bite that tongue internalize
Freedom's coming watch us rise

Meet and greet have a set
Pass the plate not discreet
Fleece the flock penetrate
Hold the line denigrate
Watch them cry no surprise
Guilty pleasure realize
Power mongers spreading lies

Sick like cancer brainwashed minds
Tippy toe egg shell lives
Bastards bleeding from their eyes
Watchful scheming rob the youth
Terror fill with partial truth
Fringe beginning holocaust
Pay your penance or be lost

The beauty within true nature's glow
The gift of our essence find it and flow

A lightness in step a body in shape
Eyes full of brightness recording a tape

Inspired by wisdom humble and wise
Laughter and freedom what a surprise

The pain it took to arrive at this place
Might be the tool to save our whole race

Free will is good humility better
Clear conscience is freedom wisdom be clever

Hidden inside the holiest of all places
Upright on two legs a species with faces

Each with a gift to share with this earth
It was seen coming since our first birth

Tested and hardened willing to die
On to the next life, blink of an eye

Where am I at I know where I'm from
This earth is amazing except for its scum

The liars still lying 2000 years
Enslaving the conquered stifled by fears

Murderous demons soulless in God
Greedy intentions looks like a fraud

Deft dumb and blind claiming holy in faith
The blood of the murdered could fill a large lake

What no one's watching are you insane
Rotten and soulless the church is the blame

Cesspool of righteous acts of disgust
Dilutional purpose sick from the dust

Breaking the spirit stealing the soul
Sheep with no meaning sneaky and bold

A light in the dak leads to the heart

A sound from the earth will lead to new birth

A color in the sky will teach you to fly

A touch of the breeze souths panic of knees

A rush of new growth may reveal life's true oath

A hawk in the tree might set your mind free

A smell of a flower could give you true power

A source of a stream may lead to the dream

A will of the true is what I will do

Blended reality cosmic fate
Rest in peace without hate

Riding waves wings a loft
Feeling sound heart that's soft

Willing waiting travel time
Reaching out with this rhyme

Happy holding onto life
Good deeds doing feels so right

Silent seeking truth prevails
Endless talking spike like nails

Mystic music without end
Dancing angels are as friend

Conscious caring hold the light
Is worth knowing why I fight

Fight for freedom free your soul
Surrender ego cosmic roll

Misled tragic chaos addicted
Anxiety ridden mind all twisted

Societal norm treated with drugs
Bigots bending never hugs

Treasonous tendencies justification holly
Main stream media dark rotten bully

Taking like fools dead bent dark souls
Slithering the earth living in holes

Rock its foundation under mind control
Power mad hungry playing its roll

Ignorant condition humanities lies
Cancerous demons dead darkened eyes

Massive distractions hiding our truth
Look to the universe to find your proof

Designed to deceive toils of fools
Lift up your head find your own tools

Calibrating calculating perfecting a craft
Alone on the ocean safe in a raft

Eating up wisdom discarding lies
Building up stamina reading the eyes

Dilutions faded covered with love
Peaceful solutions at hand from above

Worth every moment worth any strain
No matter how bad this hurts my small brain

Not even asking why me this time
Sword is sharpened new scabbard divine

Dense fog has lifted giving me hope
Love is worth living eyes on the pope

Feeble and useless a weak empire dies
Start at the top a creature snake eyes

Hire your mersons pay plundered lute
I'll be on my mountain playing my flute

Amuse me I don't remember why
I have to walk and birds get to fly

Why feet and not wings
I don't agree with everything

Why not a tail like a fish in the water
Why ask the question why even bother

So many questions so little time
Why doesn't mankind know how to shine

What was the purpose why all the traps
Sick sense of humor the answer perhaps

Nothing seems right nothing seems wrong
Intense intuition free from the throng

Okay fine what will be next
I need some guidance not another text

Hug me kiss me return my stair
Love me undress me 'till I'm bare

Cosmic collision some call it fate
I remember last time and it was great

End means beginning that's how it goes
Tingle inside me that's how I know

But keep denying your only true self
Like layers of lettuce expired on the shelf

Maybe the core will be okay
Maybe not who's to say

Only you know through free will it's found
Change is coming earth shaking profound

Ignorance no longer hurray I'm now free
The cliff had a bottom thank goodness for me

Badgered and held back told eyes insane
When I first woke up it was through pain

This time was love clarity so clear
Committed to truth never in fear

Loveless in love fearless in fear
What are the answers why are we here

Give me a purpose show me the way
Free me from all of the words that they say

Clawing and biting tearing me down
Only escape the earth's sacred ground

Why so much ugly why so much pain
Nothing make sense except sun and the rain

What about trust where did it go
Where is the honor I do not know

Lonely and lost addictions galore
Ism's are everywhere cannot ignore

Narratives lying to cover up lies
Stealing our goodness poisoning our eyes

Where is the thanks where's the respect
The things we can't buy with any blank check

The once scared soul I use to have
Is now alive and giving back

It's misguided mangled ways
Are now the past that's where they'll stay

Turning anger into love
Feeding fear piece from above

No switch to flip conditioned primed
It's our time to rip and rhyme

Freely floating here and there
Aware of wisdom in the air

This energy so intense
Leaves me laughing don't make sense

A heart's true message from divine
Feathers tickle lets me shine

Blend the ice stir the soul
It is time to let it go

No one shall see the guiding force
The healed heart yours of course

The battles won you're free to fly
Just remember when and why

Hold your light out let it shine
Light the path for all to find

Caress the wisdom hold it dear
Someday soon it will be clear

Test the water don't get burned
Use everything you've lived and learned

You got this child as wild as you are
Raise the conscience near and far

Harbinger of bread that keep me fed
Tucks me into bed again

Heralding wholeness piece at last
Only forward never back

Gotcha moment tingle spine
Embrace the light and let it shine

Cosmic horns sounding off
Preachers bleeding from their cough

Instant brilliance mesmerized
Watch the love dissolve the lies

Bitter apple take a bite
Denial will not win this fight

Hostile acts no longer reign
There's no room they are insane

Check your conscience look inside
Are you ready for the ride

Like kids crave candy adults crave drugs
Doctors say take this to get rid of your bugs

Pharmaceutical suicide gimme a break
Look in the mirror and see a fake

Each answer we have take a look around
Opinions controlling without a sound

Chemical plants instead of the natural
Big pharma money life support critical

Nose ring inserted chain attached
Chemically dependent time to detach

Get your shit straight figure it out
Don't let big pharma string you out

The spark the seed the one we need

The power the shower we need it each hour

The kiss the caress the sexy black dress

The door the key the feeling of free

The random the purpose what lives on the surface

The refined the sublime the changing of mind

The denial the pain the butchery brain

The heart the spine how long 'til we shine

The breath the wind there is no sin

The fear the shame who is to blame

The corrupt the greed feeding off seed

The answer the glory write down your own story

The brave the path guided from rath

Heart in one hand mind in the other
Why do they fight like me and a brother

Where is my piece where is the still
Where is the top of this great hill

Carry me home the finish line
But first give me piece so that I can shine

Wipe off my tears make me strong
Send an angel with her song

Guide my path shine your light
So that I can sleep at night

Keep me close never far
Bless me hold me shooting star

Life is worth living happy and free
Love is my purpose so shall it be

Static state memories real
Not from this body alternate field

Bought and paid for through the pain
Here for good never wane

Always forward never back
Locomotion clear the track

Slow and steady rest required
Shooting star burning fire

Filters gone strainer full
Dump the waste continue roll

Discern the truth cast aside
What doesn't fit hopeless pride

Wars insane when piece is real
Drop the righteous love appeal

Wreckless acts purpose power
Time to take a real cold shower

Bigger than life taking hold
Me my master never cold

Lifted in laughter guided by love
Shoe on each foot wings of the dove

Concurring karma universe awaits
No more candy no more cakes

Confidence growing burning fire
Charged up energy one big desire

Silent mind glowing heart
Healthy body smelly fart

Ticket punched on the ride
Answer calling no fear inside

Dignity breeding valve based
Comb my hair wash my face

Reflection glowing who is that
Do not know who's staring back

Without false pride love yourself
It's up to you your own health

We deserve to know our own love
It is given from above

Follow the heart it does not lie
If not controlled or despised

It's your life it belongs to you
No one's opinion should cause you blue

We know ourselves we have a job
Trust our hearts don't be a snob

Are we equal yes we are
Gifted beings find your card

Time to shine here and now
Find your pearl and refine

Progress forward never back
Cargo caring on the track

Conjuring up bridging gaps
Testing theories blasting caps

Mystic beginning vision love
Duality needed to discove

Hardly fun worth the pain
Piece inside not in vain

Honest honor prudent pride
Dignity respect high end ride

Wrestling wrangling truth revealed
Whistles blowing conscience sealed

Negative out positive in
Head held high strength within

Brought from cosmos lift the vail
Fine tune sight cannot fail

I am broken please set me free
No more pain and misery

Let me learn, why this is so
Hold my hand so I can grow

Wash my anger down the drain
I can't take it, no more pain

Replace my guilt with only love
Free me guide me fill my glove

Show me light give me trust
Take my shame so I don't bust

Cleanse my spirit heal my soul
Let the negativity all go

Past and present merge as one
Cut the shackles so I can run

Respect the process we are great
Make an appointment, don't be late

What about the horse, did it drink
or was it ignorant on the brink

Was it blinded by it's faith
Or embrace a brand new way

Could it envision what went wrong
Or did it receive its old song

It was weary, this we know
Spirit too weak to pull the plow

In its fear, it's lashed out
Horrified of death began to pout

Poor old me worked 'til death
No I don't want another breath

The spring of life passed on by
Eyes a blur began to cry

What a waste, refused to drink
Ignorance leading us to the brink

Permanently numb big pharma drugs
Trained professionals acting like thugs

Side effects many amount
To future ills immune account

Not our fault look the other way
Accountability signed away

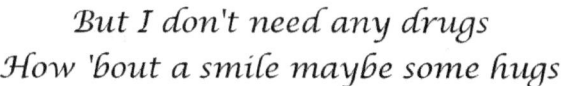

Full blow racket keeping you sick
I'd rather smoke weed with a bic

But I don't need any drugs
How 'bout a smile maybe some hugs

Too damn easy laying it down
Making power look the clown

Irritating it might seem
Not as bad as the queen

Rather be dead than return
To a life of no concern

Hear that inner child screaming in your ear
Sick and tired of living in conformity and fear

Burdens blocking obligations
Opinions swirl intense sensation

All a figment of your mind
The one that's left us deaf and blind

Pushing power get 'em young
Destroying gifts acts of scam

False in ego black as night
Waging war in delight

Darkness creeping all around
Soulless zealots making sound

Back to blackmail cuz it works
Holding secrets danger lurks

Desperately destroying any light
But not this time I know I'm right

My carnation get off my cloud
And yes I like the music loud

Chaos and confusion beneath my wings
Humans and their crazy things

Crutches gone don't need a crux
Now it's time to earn those bucks

Predictable rival head low for survival

Not much chance to learn this new dance

But there is hope
Some will embrace this dope

Keep on moving not moving on
Never a bore no time to yawn

Past the point no return
Stepping up it's my yearn

So damn easy clowning around
Such a precious lovely sound

Arrogant idiots triangular cause
Obeyed by corrupted laws

In the name of power pay you dues
Concept created long before jews

Material wealth preoccupied
Robbing blindly in front of our eyes

Holding itself above the laws
Hold on a minute cuz here comes jaws

Take your power and shove it in that place
I'll give you help to make more space

Sick and tired worn out and weary
Yep I exist in my own theory

Free to examine rights and wrongs
Without opinion from ding dongs

Never waning focus clear
Got my mission why I'm here

Protect my children keep them safe
While I slay the fangs of faith
Feed them cloth them keep them warm
Know them free them from the swarm
You 'da king the only light

Made of love to win this fight
Hostage takers strike them down
Show this world you not clowning around
Break new bread baked in love
Send evil running with one big shove
They know who they are so do you
Undeserving of life's stew
I'll do my best please watch my back
Make sure my train don't jump the track

Who is the terrorist who gives us fear
Please speak up so all can hear

Please define this scary word
And make sure to inform the herd

Only want credit for what's good
Salvation sickness has withstood

Deaf in denial lopped another head
History filled with cowardly dread

Keeps on repeating wonder why
Look in the mirror then start to cry

Fooled again smoke and mirrors
Another lifetime living with fears

This time I'm coming ain't gonna stop
Topple the tower from bottom to top

Ruled by love energy
Not by hate and misery

Put on my pants just like you
Nothing fancy nothing to prove

No shrine needed no power play
Existing only day by day

Humble enough to know my place
Resilient enough to win each race

Alchemizing what makes sense
In this land of the dense

Dense in concept creativity slim
Wrapped up in a dying skin

Was a good run of dirty lies
On the horizon a big surprise

Just a warning not to late
Stop denying the human fate

Seeing the planet through spiritual eyes
Will surely help you realize
Turn off the tv put down your phone
This was provided it's our home
Create the star you feel her vibe
She's alive and will survive

Learning her secrets awake and live
Broken free from the hive

Teleported across her face
Touched emotions from this grace

Parachuted back to earth
Back to madness and men who birth

Man knows better men don't care
What is stolen or who they scare

Intuition high alert
Just say no dessert

Plump little piggies waddle by
In their mouth another pie

What respect wow what pride
It's a gene doctors cried

Fat excuses for failed fitness
Look around all the witness

Fast food Friday everyday
Hustle bustle doesn't pay

Don't expect in return
The respect you didn't earn

Lethargic and lazy not aware
Even after the health scare

Codependent on big med
Cuz you won't get out of bed

What a life I won't judge
But maybe loose a little pudge

Same old path same old story
Twisted past horror glory

Made up laws made up rules
Conformity life of the fools

Another victim another loss
Of the power's proclaimed boss

Shady secrets shady creed
Stop at nothing lust and greed

Big influence big in wealth
Not concerned with true health

Buying in selling out
Broken system without doubt

Sad inside sad without
Cut from source fear to shout

Wake up people get rebirthed
Support the mother we call earth

Acting the bomb
Living a cracker

Wounded worrier
Not a slacker

Lifted in conscience
But not high enough

To see through the smoke screen
And all the guff

Energy pulled this way and that
Vampires lurking black like a cat

Pressure release purge required
Torch in hand to light that fire

It will take time and dedication
But you will be free to relish in elation

Take my hand be yourself
Don't become another elf

To stand alone is our right
And is worth an emotional fight

Feeling torn ripped apart
Whatever feels bad let it depart

Complete a cycle clear your past
Don't let disaster ever last

Be your light meant for each
Feel your toes out on that beach

Conflicting opinions what's right or wrong
Exist through heart and its truth song

Break tradition adjust your sail
Start migration like the whale

Negative to positive fear can't win
If it does we start again

My last turn no more line
Letting light out enough to blind

Good time girl on the mend
Looking for love and a friend

Healer inside her crying out
Overcoming opinion facing doubt

Child like innocence with horns of a bull
There will be no pulling of wool

Natural beauty compassion filled
Plenty of energy without pills

Appreciation tuning in
Wanting freedom from within

Vail lifted chaos averted
With that death she had flirted

Conformity awareness figuring out
What's right for her a path without doubt

But in her heart she will always shine
No matter the clutter or the rhyme

A truly gifted natural force
Will find her way this of course

No more fine only great
Full of pride cleared the slate

New beginning opportunity knocks
Foundation built on concrete blocks

No more head games based on lies
Honesty is worth the tries

Just keep trying don't give up
Soon your gift will fill your cup

Buckle down sit up straight
Clam your glory life is great

So proud there are no words
Free to roam without the herds

Sovereignty claimed for the self
Don't give a damn to be an elf

Unique in love riding a wave
Giving all the she was gave

Roo don't forget adulthood is a trap
They're not me and you they don't know crap

DAUGHTER I NEVER HAD

Rest easy my daughter lay away doubt
I am so sorry we had to shout

Never a father only a dad
Now I know why you are sad

here to support, guide and love
You are my angel from above

Rest without fear burden is mine
Find your inner child and let her blind

Walk in the presence show the whole world
Here to catch when you twirl

You have my word I'm charged for good
Fatherly love is now understood

Be the princess you've dreamed of
My full support because of our love

Book Review
Jonah Meyer

"Hold out your hand she said to me I am the magic you are the key"

The roughly seventy-five pages in this collection of free-flowing, expansive poetry touch on a rich array of diverse, universal themes. Several topics are explored through the poet's imagination and served up fresh, like a delicious meal for readers of inspired verse. These include, among other subjects, the feminine nature and spirit of beauty, music of a multitude of instruments, love and its discontents, God's abundant universe, getting back up when life throws one down to the ground, grace, and sin, shining free with growth, healthy questioning of those in authority (who often act with ulterior, fear-spreading motives), and so much more. GoForth is not new to the game of producing thought-provoking, sprawling collections of poetry, and this book, like his others, has much to offer.

Written in the author's usual style and method, this is not a "traditional" poetry collection wherein there is a set number of distinct poems, each titled and self-contained. Rather, the entire relatively short collection can—and likely should—be read and taken in as one long, thoughtful flow of continuous poetic exploration. Consisting entirely of two-lined couplets, complete with the pleasing music of end-rhyme, the one exception to this format is the final piece entitled "Daughter I Never Had." Here, GoForth expresses a heartbreakingly beautiful communication to his child, acknowledging in retrospect an absence of fatherly connection while simultaneously expressing guidance, love, and support. The poet encourages his daughter to embrace her 'inner child," telling her to "Be the princess you've dreamed of," and letting her know in no uncertain terms that he is here to catch her when she twirls. The sentiment GoForth evokes with this poem—much like the rest of the book's entirety—is humbling, graceful, and true to the heart.

www.ingramcontent.com/pod-product-compliance
Lightning Source LLC
LaVergne TN
LVHW010604070526
838199LV00063BA/5067